The Frog Who Stirred the Cream

A Russian Folk Tale

Retold by Evelyn Stone

Illustrated by Jesse Dugan Sweetwater

HAMPTON-BROWN

Characters

**Lyagushka
(La-GOOSH-ka)**

The grasshopper

One day, Lyagushka jumps into a pail of cream. How will she get out?

The Frog Who Stirred the Cream

One day, Lyagushka hopped into my yard.

Lyagushka jumped over to a pail.
Of course, she wanted to look into it!

Lyagushka jumped up and landed inside the pail. SPLASH!

Cool, white cream covered Lyagushka. It covered her legs. It covered her back. It even covered her tiny nose.

Don't worry! Lyagushka loved to swim.

♪ Song In the Cream

She jumped. She landed.

She jumped and landed.

She jumped and landed
   in the cream.

She played. She splashed.

She played and splashed.

She played and splashed
   in the cream.

12

Lyagushka paddled this way and that. She kicked and splashed and paddled some more. She paddled faster and faster.

She was very happy!

Finally Lyagushka stopped swimming. She was ready to get out.

Lyagushka tried to jump. She tried and tried, but she could not get out. The pail was too deep!

Is This the End?

Poor Lyagushka, poor Lyagushka,
    paddled in a pail.
First she loved it.
Then she hated it.
Is this the end of her tale?

Poor Lyagushka, poor Lyagushka,
    paddled in a pail.
First she smiled.
Then she frowned.
Is this the end of her tale?

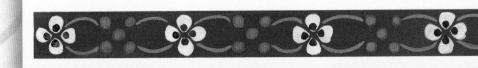

Then Lyagushka had an idea. She decided to climb up the side of the pail. She climbed and she climbed.

Do you think she got out?

No! Lyagushka slipped back down. She climbed up again. She slipped down again. Lyagushka could not climb out!

Lyagushka started to worry. She decided
to call for help. Lyagushka called and called
and CALLED!

Well, no one helped Lyagushka. And she was so tired. She started to sink!

But Lyagushka did not give up. She kicked hard, and she bobbed back up.

Lyagushka dropped down again. She kicked
back up. Then she dropped back down.

Suddenly, Lyagushka touched something with
her foot. It was a lump on the bottom of the pail!
She stepped on the lump. She jumped off it.
PLOP! She landed on the grass.

At first Lyagushka did not know what happened.
Then she figured it out. That lump was butter. Lyagushka
kicked and turned the cream into butter!

♪ Song A Happy Day

I dropped into a pail of cream.

I trapped myself inside.

I bobbed, I dipped,

I slipped, I dripped.

I grabbed onto the side.

I stirred and kicked

And whipped the cream.

It turned into a lump.

I stepped on it

And hopped right out.

I'm glad that I can jump!

And the butter tasted good, too!